4 Weeks of Fabulous Paleolithic Breakfasts

by Amelia Simons

Other Books by Amelia Simons

Complete Paleo Meals: A Paleo Cookbook Featuring Paleo Comfort Foods

Gluten-Free Slow Cooker: Easy Recipes for a Gluten Free Diet

Paleolithic Slow Cooker Soups and Stews: Healthy Family Gluten-Free Recipes

Paleo Slow Cooker: Simple and Healthy Gluten-Free Recipes

Going Paleolithic: A Quick Start Guide for a Gluten-Free Diet

4 Weeks of Fabulous Paleolithic Dinners

4 Weeks of Fabulous Paleolithic Lunches

The Ultimate Paleolithic Collection

4 MORE Weeks of Fabulous Paleolithic Breakfasts

Table of Contents

A Little Taste of the Paleo Lifestyle

What is Paleo? The Paleo way of eating includes various names like: Primal Diet, Cave Man Diet, Stone Age Diet, Hunter-Gatherer Diet, the Paleo Diet ™ and a few others. Basically, it consists of a low-carb diet that attempts to imitate what our ancestors ate before farming and other advancements changed our diets.

As with many other ways of eating, there is some variation and degrees of limitations practiced by those who try to eat as our "primal" ancestors did. With that said, what follows are the basic guidelines that most proponents of the Paleolithic way of eating agree upon.

Whether or not you fully embrace this way of eating by going "cold turkey," or ease your way gently into the program, here are some basic guidelines.

What foods are "off limits?"

Refined sugars: The rule is to avoid all sugars. These include white sugar, high fructose corn syrup, candy, milk chocolate, soda, and artificial sweeteners. Some spokespersons for Paleolithic allow small amounts of raw honey, pure maple syrup, and coconut sugar, but also advise these sugars to be an occasional treat.

Grains: The types of grain to avoid include wheat, rye, barley, rice, oats and corn. Foods would include bread, pasta, baked goods, pancakes, biscuits, muffins, bagels, and cereals. Grains are high in carbohydrates and are calorie-dense.

Legumes: This category includes beans of all kinds, peas, lentils, soybeans, tofu, soy products, and peanuts.

Dairy products: Try to exclude eating dairy products like regular milk, butter, cream, fruit yogurts, ice cream, and processed cheeses.

- While many Paleolithic eaters do not eat dairy, others do. If you can tolerate dairy and want to enjoy it on occasion, start with cultured butter, Greek yogurt (not fruit flavored), kefir, clotted milks, and aged cheeses. These are fermented products that drastically reduce the lactose (milk sugar) levels.

- Next would come raw, high-fat dairy like raw butter and cream because they are minimally processed and are good sources of saturated fat. Most of these are free from lactose and casein and should come from grass-fed, pasture-fed animals.

- Avoid homogenized and pasteurized milk. If you must buy it, make it organic, hormone and antibiotic-free milk. Because nuts are allowed, consider substituting unsweetened almond milk and coconut milk in place of cow's milk.

- Grass-fed butter is considered okay on occasion. If you want to eat cheese on occasion, too, be sure they are aged cheeses because aging drastically reduces the levels of lactose and casein.

Some meats: Avoid processed meats like hot dogs, bologna, and lunchmeats. If eating bacon and sausage, try to eat those without nitrates and nitrites. The bacon issue is still widely debated among the Paleo community—some believe it is okay if using nitrite/nitrate free bacon that is also sugar-free. Others believe because it is cured, it is not allowed. YOU DECIDE!

Oils: Avoid anything "partially hydrogenated," shortening, margarines, canola oil, soybean oil, cottonseed oil, peanut oil, corn oil, and sunflower oil. Note: be sure to check the label on your mayonnaise.

What foods are allowed?

Meats, seafood and eggs: Meats, seafood, and eggs are perhaps the most important components of the Paleolithic Diet. These include beef, pork, lamb, bison, poultry, shrimp, crab, trout, salmon, mackerel, along with other wild-caught fish, including sardines, oysters, mussels, and clams. Once again, bacon and sausage is widely debated so you decide if it is okay for you or not.

Vegetables: Vegetables are greatly encouraged and can be eaten in unlimited quantities. Focus on leafy greens of all kinds. Whether or not to include potatoes and other starchy tubers in your diet is an area of varying opinions at this point.

Fruits: Fruits are allowed but should be limited, especially if you need to lose weight. High sugar fruits like dried fruits and juices should be eaten only occasionally.

Nuts and seeds: Nuts and seeds are generally allowed. They are high in fat so limit your intake if you want to lose weight. Nuts and seeds include macadamias, Brazil nuts, hazelnuts, pistachios, walnuts, almonds, pecans, cashews, squash seeds, sunflower seeds, and pumpkin seeds. Note: Peanuts are legumes and are not allowed.

Healthy fats: Olive oil and nut oils like coconut oil are generally encouraged. Butter, palm oil, ghee, and animal fats are on the allowable list.

Beverages: All spokespersons agree that water is best and should be your main drink. Generally, tea is considered to be fine, while there continues to be some variations concerning coffee and alcohol. Beverages that require sweeteners by sugars or artificial sweeteners are discouraged.

Throughout this collection of recipes (and the others in my series), I have tried to guide you into this way of eating. The goal is to make positive changes toward this way of eating without making you feel like it has to be one certain way. Simply know your labels and use your best judgment.

If you can't afford organic or grass-fed beef, don't fret about that. Just buy the basic ingredients and follow the basic guidelines for eating Paleolithic style.

I hope you enjoy this collection of Paleolithic recipes. They are some of my family's absolute favorites and I hope they will become some of your favorites, too!

FRITTATAS

&

EGG DISHES

Garden Fresh Frittata

Frittatas are a warm, satisfying way to start your day. A frittata is a large, flat Italian-style omelet baked in the oven. Frittatas are sliced and served to a large group of people (5-8). They are great for leftovers and quick lunches, too.

Ingredients:

- 8 eggs

- ¼ cup almond milk

- Salt and pepper to taste

- 2 tablespoons olive oil

- 2 to 3 garlic cloves, finely chopped or crushed

- 2 cups baby spinach, chopped or shredded

- 1 red onion, chopped

- ½ cup fresh mushrooms, sliced

- 1 red bell pepper, sliced or chunked

- 2 tablespoons fresh parsley, if desired

Directions:

1. Preheat your oven to 425 degrees.

2. In a separate bowl, combine the eggs and almond milk.

3. Mix well and set aside.

4. Place an oven-safe medium-sized skillet over medium heat and pour in the olive oil.

5. Once the oil is heated, place the garlic, spinach, red onion, fresh mushrooms and red bell pepper into the skillet.

6. Cook the vegetables for 3-4 minutes until they are tender.

7. Slowly add in the egg/almond mixture to the vegetables in the skillet and turn the heat down to low.

8. Cook over low heat for approximately 10 minutes.

9. Once the edges look firm, place the oven-safe skillet into your preheated oven.

10. Cook in a 425 degree oven for 15-20 minutes.

11. The frittata will be done when the center is firm and no longer jiggles.

12. Top the frittata with fresh parsley and cut into wedges.

13. Serve hot and enjoy.

Veggie Frittata

This fresh tasting egg dish is a great all-in-one meal. The bright collection of vegetables makes it an attractive choice for brunch.

Ingredients:

- 1 cup broccoli florets diced into small pieces

- ½ cup chopped red onion

- 1 yellow summer squash, diced

- 1 cup cooked meat diced into small pieces

- ½ cup sun dried tomatoes, chopped

- 7 eggs

- Salt and pepper to taste

- Coconut oil for frying

Directions:

1. Preheat your oven to 375 degrees F.

2. In the bottom of a 10-inch oven-proof frying pan, melt enough coconut oil to cover the bottom.

3. Place the broccoli and onions in the frying pan and cook until the onions are translucent.

4. Now add the squash, meat, and sun dried tomatoes and cook gently until the squash is tender.

5. Now spread the mixture around the bottom of the frying pan evenly.

6. In a bowl, whisk together the eggs until thoroughly blended and pour them over the mixture in the frying pan.

7. Cook over medium low heat until you see the eggs firming up along the edge of the pan.

8. Place the frying pan into your preheated oven and cook for 10-12 minutes.

9. The frittata is done when the middle is firm.

South of the Border Frittata

Serve up a little spice and excitement with your eggs. This satisfying dish is an excellent treat any time.

Ingredients:

- 1 tablespoon coconut oil
- ¼ cup onion, finely chopped
- 1 jalapeno pepper, chopped with seeds removed
- 1 pound ground beef
- 1 cup grated raw sweet potato
- 2 garlic cloves, minced
- 1 tablespoons chili powder
- 1 teaspoon ground cumin
- ½ cup unsweetened salsa
- 12 eggs
- Salt and pepper to taste

Directions:

1. Preheat your oven to 350 degrees F.

2. In a large frying pan, sauté the onions and jalapeno in the coconut oil until the onions are tender.

3. Add the ground beef and cook just until it starts to brown.

4. Add the potato and garlic to the frying pan.

5. Cook until the beef is completely browned and the sweet potato is soft.

6. Add the chili powder, cumin, and salsa

7. Stir in the spices and salsa and heat through.

8. At this point, taste the mixture and season with salt and pepper as desired.

9. Remove from heat and transfer the meat mixture to an 11" × 7" glass-baking dish.

10. Spread the meat mixture evenly over the bottom of the glass pan.

11. In a separate mixing bowl, break open the eggs and beat together thoroughly.

12. Pour the eggs over the meat mixture in the baking dish.

13. Cover the glass pan with aluminum foil.

14. Bake in a 350 degree oven for 30 minutes.

15. After 30 minutes, remove the foil and bake for an additional 10-15 minutes--until the eggs are set in the middle when you jiggle the pan.

16. Once firmness is achieved, remove from the oven and allow to cool briefly.

17. Cut into serving sizes and enjoy.

Quiche Cups

Now you can enjoy healthy crustless quiché everyday. These breakfast cups can also be stored in the refrigerator until they are ready to be reheated and eaten at a later date.

Ingredients:

- ½ pound of meat (ground pork or turkey works well)

- 1 cup of vegetables of your choosing: chopped spinach, scallions or onions, fresh mushrooms, or bell peppers

- ⅓ cup shredded cheese (optional. Make it **aged** cheese)

- 5 eggs

- ¾ cup almond or coconut milk

Directions:

1. Preheat your oven to 325 degrees F.

2. Grease a muffin tin with olive oil.

3. Cook the meat of your choice and drain if necessary, then set aside.

4. Next, sauté the vegetables until they are tender.

5. Place the sautéed vegetables and cheese in a bowl and mix together. Now set aside.

6. Whisk together the eggs and milk and pour equal amounts of batter into each cup of a greased muffin tin.

7. Add desired amount of meat and veggie/cheese mixture to each muffin cup.

8. Bake for 20-25 minutes or until golden brown.

9. Briefly allow to cool.

10. Remove muffins from pan and enjoy.

Turkey & Eggs

Spicy ground turkey patties and eggs sunny side up. Unique, filling, and delicious.

Ingredients:

- ½ pound ground turkey
- 3 tablespoons finely chopped onions
- 2 teaspoons coconut aminos
- ½ teaspoon cayenne pepper
- ½ teaspoon garlic powder
- 1 teaspoon sea salt
- 1 teaspoon black pepper
- Coconut oil or spray for frying
- 4 eggs

Directions:

1. In a large bowl, combine the turkey, onions, aminos, cayenne pepper, garlic powder, salt, and pepper.
2. Mix until all the ingredients are blended together.
3. Form this mixture into four patties.
4. Place a large skillet over medium heat and place just enough coconut oil or spray to coat the pan.
5. Place the four patties into the frying pan.

6. Cook for about 5 minutes and then turn the patties over.

7. Heat for an additional 5 minutes, until the patties have cooked thoroughly.

8. Set this pan aside or remove the patties so you can proceed with the same pan for the next step.

9. In a heated frying pan, carefully crack one egg at a time, doing your best to keep the egg in a rounded shape. This works best when your pan is hot.

10. Cover the frying pan and cook for 3-5 minutes—until the egg whites are no longer runny.

11. Remove the eggs when they are done and place one egg on top of a meat patty.

12. Top with salt and pepper as desired.

Chili Crepes

A fun and filling twist on traditional crepes. Ground beef and diced veggies with a kick make this egg wrap-up something to remember.

Ingredients:

- ¼ cup water

- ¼ cup each of onions, mushrooms, red and green peppers. Dice these for cooking

- 1 pound lean ground beef

- ½ teaspoon salt

- ¼ teaspoon garlic powder

- ½ teaspoon chili powder

- 1½ teaspoon coconut aminos

- Black pepper

- 3 tablespoons of green onions, diced to use as a garnish

Crepe

- 3 eggs

- ¼ cup coconut flour

- ½ cup almond or coconut milk

- ¼ cup water

- Dash of salt

Directions:

1. In a large heated skillet, add the water, onions, mushrooms, and red and green peppers.

2. Heat on high until onions become tender which will take about 7 to 8 minutes.

3. Now break up the meat and combine it into the vegetable mixture.

4. Add in the salt, garlic powder, chili powder, aminos, and black pepper.

5. Continue over medium heat, stirring occasionally, until the meat is cooked through.

6. Take the beef mixture and scoop it into a bowl and set aside.

7. Now it's time to start your crepes.

8. Whisk all the ingredients for the crepes together in a large bowl.

9. Be sure to break up any clumps of flour as you mix ingredients together.

10. Heat a skillet on the top of your stove and grease lightly with coconut oil.

11. Pour about ¼ cup of your crepe batter into your pan and swirl the batter around to evenly coat the pan.

12. Heat on medium-high heat until you begin to notice tiny bubbles forming throughout the crepe.

13. The sides of the crepe should also become golden brown in color.

14. With a soft spatula, carefully lift the crepe from the pan and place it on a plate large enough to accommodate the crepe.

15. Fill the crepe with the meat mixture by placing it down the middle of the crepe.

16. Top the meat mixture with the green onions.

17. Fold one end over the mixture and begin to roll as you tuck the sides into the middle.

18. Serve with fresh fruit.

Red Pepper & Arugula Omelet

The colorful contrast in this dish is mirrored in its bright combination of flavors.

Ingredients:

- Coconut oil for frying
- 1 onion, sliced
- 1 red pepper, chopped
- 1 cup chopped arugula
- 1 tomato, chopped
- 4 eggs, beaten
- Salt and pepper to taste
- Juice from one lemon

Directions:

1. In a frying pan, place a small amount of coconut oil and turn the stovetop burner up to medium heat.

2. Once the oil is heated, add the sliced onions and cook them until they become translucent.

3. Next add the chopped bell peppers and sauté them until they are slightly soft.

4. Drop in the arugula and chopped tomato and mix well.

5. Sauté the ingredients for about three minutes.

6. Pour in the scrambled eggs and continue to stir well until the eggs are cooked through.

7. Remove from the pan and place on a plate.

8. Drizzle fresh lemon juice over the top if you like.

B.B.C. Frittata

The classic combination of bacon and broccoli simply cannot be beat. While bacon is still debated among the Paleo community, you decide if this recipe is for you or not. The addition of aged shredded cheese makes it complete if you can tolerate dairy.

Ingredients:

- ½ pound bacon, cooked and crumbled (nitrite/nitrate free)

- 1 stalk of broccoli (florets only, broken into small pieces)

- 8 eggs

- 1½ cups coconut milk

- 1 tablespoon ghee or butter, melted

- ½ cup aged shredded cheese

- Salt and pepper to taste

- Coconut oil for frying

Directions:

1. Preheat your oven to 425 degrees F. (This recipe requires a frying pan that can be placed in your oven.)

2. Cook bacon on your stovetop in a frying pan or microwave it until desired crispiness is achieved.

3. Cut the florets off the head of the broccoli and tenderize them in a microwave dish or on the stovetop in boiling water for 4 to 5 minutes.

4. In a separate bowl, whisk together the eggs, coconut milk, butter, salt, and pepper.

5. Now stir in the broccoli and crumbled bacon.

6. Pour the mixture into a frying pan that has a small amount of coconut oil melted in it.

7. Cook over medium heat until the sides of the frittata begin to firm up.

8. Remove from your stovetop and sprinkle the frittata with the shredded cheese (optional).

9. Place the entire frying pan into your preheated oven.

10. Cook for 15-20 minutes until the center of the frittata is firm.

11. Remove from the oven and allow to rest for 5 to 10 minutes.

12. Cut into wedges and enjoy.

Savory Breakfast Casserole

A quick and satisfying dish to start your morning. Using cooked meat and fresh vegetables make this casserole easy to put together.

Ingredients:

- 6 eggs

- ¼ pound cooked meat of your choice

- ¼ cup fresh sliced mushrooms

- 3 tablespoons chopped onions

- 1 teaspoon each of salt and pepper

- ½ teaspoon garlic powder

- ½ teaspoon paprika

- ½ teaspoon dried thyme

- Aged shredded cheese for topping (optional)

Directions:

1. Preheat your oven to 350 degrees F.

2. In a large bowl, combine all the ingredients except the cheese you will use as a topping and mix until all the ingredients are thoroughly blended.

3. Pour mixture into a greased 8" × 8" baking dish.

4. Sprinkle the top of the batter with shredded cheese (optional).

5. Place in preheated oven and bake for 45 minutes.

6. Slice and serve.

Zucchini Pork Casserole

Part casserole, part frittata, this dish is hearty and delicious without feeling too heavy.

Ingredients:

- 1 red onion, chopped

- 4 garlic cloves, minced

- 8 eggs

- 2 cups cooked shredded pork

- 1 zucchini, peeled and shredded

- 2 tablespoons fresh basil

- Salt and pepper to taste

- ½ - 1 cup shredded aged cheese (optional)

Directions:

1. Preheat your oven to 350 degrees F.

2. Sauté your onion and garlic in a frying pan over medium heat until the onion starts to caramelize.

3. Turn off the heat and allow the onion to remain in the pan.

4. In a mixing bowl, combine the eggs, shredded pork, shredded zucchini, basil, salt and pepper and mix until thoroughly blended.

5. Add in the sautéed onion and garlic and blend well.

6. In a greased 9" x 13" baking pan, pour the mixture into the baking dish and distribute evenly.

7. Top with shredded cheese if desired.

8. Place the dish into your oven and cook for approximately 30 minutes. Test the center for doneness

9. If you want the top to be browned, you can place the dish under the broiler for 4 to 5 minutes.

10. Cut and serve.

MUFFINS

&

BREADS

Hearty Morning Egg Cups

This versatile dish works well for a weekday breakfast, a tasty brunch recipe, or a hearty appetizer. This easy and quick meal can use leftover meat from last night's dinner. Leftover egg cups can be refrigerated and served later.

Ingredients:

- 1 tablespoon olive oil OR olive-oil spray

- 2 cups small cooked meat cubes

- 12 eggs

- Salt and pepper to taste

- ¼ cup aged shredded cheese (optional if you eat dairy)

- 3 tablespoons sliced chives

Directions:

1. Preheat your oven to 350 degrees F.

2. Gently wipe each muffin cup with olive oil or lightly spray the muffin cups with an olive oil spray.

3. Place a few meat cubes in the bottom of each cup.

4. Crack an egg and allow it to drop on top of the meat.

5. Continue this process until all your muffin cups are filled with an egg.

6. Season each egg cup with sea salt and pepper to your liking.

7. Top each egg with a small amount of shredded cheese and sliced chives if desired.

8. Bake for 20 minute until eggs are thoroughly cooked.

9. Remove from the muffin cups and serve warm.

Cranberry Almond Bread

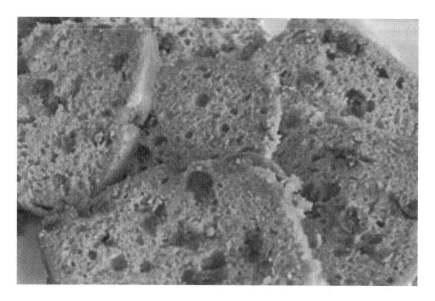

This bread is made moist with zucchini as an ingredients and is heart-healthy with the addition of almond meal and butter. Cranberries, raw honey, nut, and spices also bring lots of flavor to this tasty bread.

Ingredients:

- 4 eggs

- 2 medium zucchini, peeled and grated

- ½ cup almond butter

- 1 cup dried unsweetened cranberries

- 1 cup almond meal

- 2 tablespoons raw honey

- 1½ teaspoons cinnamon

- 1½ teaspoons nutmeg

- 1 teaspoon pumpkin pie spice

- 1 teaspoon baking soda

- ¼ teaspoon sea salt

- ¼ teaspoon ground cloves

- ¾ cup chopped walnuts

Directions:

1. Preheat your oven to 350 degrees F.

2. Prepare a 9" x 5" loaf pan with olive oil spray or apply olive oil with a paper towel.

3. Separate the egg yolks from the egg whites and put each into separate bowls.

4. Beat the egg yolks well.

5. Combine all the remaining ingredients in with the egg yolks, except for the walnuts.

6. Mix all the ingredients well.

7. In a separate bowl, whip the egg whites with an electric beater until they form stiff peaks.

8. Fold in the egg whites with the egg/zucchini mixture.

9. Gently mix in the chopped walnuts.

10. Pour the batter into your greased loaf pan.

11. Bake for 60 minutes until the top is a golden brown color.

12. Test for doneness by inserting a toothpick or cake tester in the center of the bread. It is done when only crumbs appear on the toothpick or tester.

13. Allow the bread to cool for 15-20 minutes before removing it from the pan.

14. Once it is cooled, slice to desired thickness and enjoy.

Pumpkin Gingerbread Muffins

These moist and delicious wheat-free muffins are reminiscent of warm gingerbread cookies.

Ingredients:

- ½ cup coconut flour

- 2 teaspoons ground cinnamon

- ½ teaspoon ground nutmeg

- ½ teaspoon ground ginger

- ¼ teaspoon ground cloves

- ½ teaspoon baking soda

- ½ teaspoon baking powder

- ½ teaspoon salt

- 1 cup canned 100% pureed pumpkin

- 4 eggs

- 2–3 tablespoons olive oil

- ¼ cup raw honey or pure maple syrup

- 1 teaspoon pure vanilla extract

- Pumpkin seeds or walnuts for topping (optional)

Directions:

1. Preheat your oven to 400 degrees F.

2. Lightly oil your muffin pan with coconut oil or olive oil spray.

3. In a medium-sized bowl, combine the flour, spices, soda, baking powder and salt.

4. In another bowl, pour in the pureed pumpkin.

5. Add the eggs one at a time, mixing well after each addition.

6. Add the olive oil, honey, and vanilla and mix until blended.

7. Combine the flour mixture into the pumpkin mixture and stir with a whisk until most lumps have disappeared.

8. Take a large spoon and place equal amounts into your prepared muffin pan, filling each muffin about 2/3 full.

9. Sprinkle the top of each muffin with a few seeds or walnuts if desired.

10. Place muffin tins into your preheated oven and bake for 18-20 minutes or until a tester into the middle of a muffin comes out only with crumbs—not liquid batter.

11. Allow the muffins to rest for a few minutes, then dump them out onto a wire rack to cool.

Almond Banana Bread

A moist, dense bread that's perfect for mornings or an evening treat. It is swirled with coconut, cacao powder, and pumpkin.

Ingredients:

- 1 cup almond butter
- 1 cup unsweetened shredded coconut
- 2 medium ripe bananas
- 2 eggs
- 1 teaspoon baking powder
- 1 teaspoon baking soda
- ¼ cup 100% canned pumpkin

- 3 tablespoons unsweetened cacao powder

- 1 tablespoon raw honey, if desired

Directions:

1. Preheat your oven to 350 degrees F.

2. In a mixing bowl, combine the almond butter, coconut, bananas, eggs, baking powder and soda. Be sure to mash up the bananas as best you can so it incorporates well into the batter.

3. Pour this mixture into a greased loaf pan.

4. In a separate bowl, stir together the pumpkin, cacao powder, and honey.

5. Pour this mixture down the center of the banana batter in the loaf pan and use a knife to swirl it into the batter.

6. Place the loaf pan into your preheated oven and bake for about 35-40 minutes. The center should be firm when you jiggle the pan and only crumbs should be on a toothpick or cake tester when inserted and removed.

7. Allow the bread to cool slightly before placing it on a cooling rack.

8. When cooled, slice to your desired thickness.

Cinnamon Sweet Buns

Pulled right out of the oven, these cinnamon buns are a delight.

Ingredients:

- 2–3 tablespoons coconut flour
- ¼ teaspoon baking soda
- ⅛ teaspoon sea salt
- ¼ teaspoon cinnamon
- Pinch of nutmeg
- ⅛ teaspoon pure almond extract
- 1 egg
- 2 tablespoons almond or coconut milk
- 1–2 tablespoon olive oil
- 1 tablespoon raw honey
- 1–1½ cups chopped dried fruit

Directions:

1. Preheat your oven to 375 degrees F.
2. Combine the coconut flour, baking soda, salt, cinnamon, and nutmeg in a small bowl.
3. Mix well.
4. Make a well in the center of the mixture.

5. Add the almond extract, egg, milk, oil, and honey into the well.

6. Stir thoroughly with a fork, eliminating as many lumps as possible.

7. Let the batter rest for a couple of minutes to allow the coconut flour to absorb the liquid.

8. Spoon the batter onto a parchment-lined baking sheet.

9. Spread out the batter onto the parchment-lined baking sheet and mold it into a ½-inch thick rectangle.

10. Spread dried fruit on to the top of the batter and sprinkle with cinnamon.

11. Using the edge of the parchment paper, roll up your fruit-topped batter like a cinnamon roll.

12. Bake the roll for 20-25 minutes, until the roll is golden brown.

13. Remove from oven and allow to cool briefly.

14. Slice into desired thickness and enjoy.

Banana Almond Muffins

The nutty combination of almond meal, coconut flour, and almond butter are a perfect complement to the moist bananas in the muffins.

Ingredients:

- ½ cup coconut flour

- ¼ cup almond meal

- ½ teaspoon baking powder

- ¼ teaspoon baking soda

- ⅓ cup raw honey

- Pinch of sea salt

- 4 eggs

- 1 heaping tablespoon almond butter

- 2 very ripe bananas, mashed

- 1 teaspoon pure vanilla extract

- 1 teaspoon olive or coconut oil

Directions:

1. Preheat your oven to 375 degrees F.

2. In a mixing bowl, combine the flour, almond meal, baking powder, baking soda, honey and salt.

3. In a different bowl, combine the eggs, almond butter, bananas, vanilla, and oil.

4. Slowly add the dry ingredients into the bowl with the wet ingredients and stir until the batter looks uniform in consistency.

5. Evenly divide the batter into your lightly greased muffin tins.

6. Bake in your preheated oven for 20-25 minutes.

7. Remove the muffins from the oven when cooked and allow to cool for a few minutes in the pan.

8. Dump the muffins onto a cooling rack and eat when ready.

PANCAKES

&

WAFFLES

Coconut Flour Pancakes

These wheat flour alternative pancakes are made with coconut flour. Top with your favorite fruit topping or nut butter.

Ingredients:

- 3 eggs, room temperature

- 1 teaspoon pure vanilla extract

- 1/2 cup coconut milk

- 1/4 teaspoon sea salt

- 1/2 teaspoon baking soda

- 1/3 cup coconut flour

Directions:

1. In a bowl and using a hand mixer, whip the eggs until foamy. Do this for approximately two minutes

2. Add the vanilla and milk to the eggs and mix until thoroughly blended

3. In a separate bowl, combine the salt, soda, and flour and mix thoroughly

4. Pour the flour mixture into the eggs and mix completely

5. Lightly oil a griddle with coconut oil and place over medium heat.

6. Pour a small amount of batter onto the heated griddle and spread out some with the back of your spoon

7. Cook until bubbles begin to appear in the pancake and along the sides

8. Gently flip the pancake over and cook until browned.

9. Top with your favorite topping.

Freedom Waffles

These delicious waffles are gluten free, grain-free, and dairy free. Top waffles with almond butter and fresh strawberries, blackberries or blueberries.

Ingredients:

- 2 large eggs
- ¼ cup almond or coconut milk
- 1½ cups almond flour
- 1 teaspoon sea salt
- 1 teaspoon baking soda
- Dash of cinnamon

Directions:

1. Preheat your waffle iron to your desired setting.

2. Whisk the eggs and milk together until foamy. You may find a hand mixer makes this easier.

3. Thoroughly combine all the remaining dry ingredients together in a separate bowl.

4. Add the egg/milk mixture into the bowl with the combined dry ingredients and mix until smooth.

5. Put 1/4 cup of the batter into the preheated waffle iron.

6. Cook until golden brown and then remove.

7. Top with fresh fruit of your choice and/or almond butter.

Yum!

Nutty Pancakes

These wheat-free pancakes are heart healthy and delicious. The chestnut flour and almond meal add warm and nutty undertones to these pancakes.

Ingredients:

- 1 cup chestnut flour
- ½ cup almond meal
- ⅔ cup coconut or almond milk
- 1 tablespoon raw honey (optional)
- 2 egg whites
- Coconut oil for frying

Directions:

1. Combine the flour, almond meal, milk, and honey in a bowl and mix well.

2. In a separate bowl, beat the egg whites with a hand mixer until stiff peaks form.

3. Gently fold the egg whites into the batter.

4. Place a small amount of coconut oil in a frying pan and heat over medium heat.

5. Once heated, place about two tablespoons of batter into the frying pan, or more if you like bigger pancakes.

6. Allow small bubbles to form and the sides to harden slightly, about 2 to 3 minutes, then flip the pancake.

7. Once the second side is golden brown, remove from the frying pan.

8. Serve warm and top with your favorite topping such as pure maple syrup and berries.

Fluffy Coconut Pancakes

These pancakes are enjoyably tall and fluffy. Topped with pure maple syrup or strawberries, they are impossible to resist.

Ingredients:

- 4 eggs at room temperature
- 1 cup coconut milk
- 2 teaspoons pure vanilla extract
- 1 tablespoon raw honey (optional)
- ½ cup coconut flour
- 1 teaspoon baking soda
- ½ teaspoon sea salt
- Coconut oil for frying

Directions:

1. In a bowl, whisk the eggs together well until foamy. You may want to use a hand mixer.

2. Pour in the milk, vanilla, and honey into the eggs and mix well.

3. In a separate bowl, combine flour, soda, and salt and mix well.

4. Place a frying pan or griddle on your stovetop over medium heat with enough coconut oil to just cover the bottom.

5. Once the oil is heated, pour or spoon enough batter to form your pancake.

6. Cook until the edges of the pancake start to dry and harden and bubbles form throughout the pancake.

7. Flip the pancake over and cook until golden brown.

8. Top your pancake with your favorite topping like berries and pure maple syrup.

Sweet Potato Latkes

Typically, latkes are prepared by grating raw potatoes, usually russets, as they have a high starch value. Once formed, the latkes are fried in heated oil until they are golden brown on each side. By using sweet potatoes, you avoid the high starch, yet still get to enjoy a crispy treat.

Ingredients:

- 5 cups grated sweet potato

- 2 eggs

- 2 tablespoons onions, minced

- 1 teaspoon cinnamon

- Salt and pepper to taste

- Coconut oil for frying

Directions:

1. Mix all the ingredients together in a large mixing bowl.

2. Heat a griddle or frying pan over medium heat and melt a spoonful of coconut oil.

3. Take a small amount of the potato mixture and drop it onto the hot griddle or skillet and form little cakes.

4. Cook for 3-5 minutes on each side, cooking until each side is golden brown and heated all the way through.

5. Top the latkes with favorites like fried eggs and bacon if you wish.

Apple Cinnamon Pancakes

Green apples give these pancakes a refreshing tartness. You will find they are tasty and satisfying as well.

Ingredients:

- ½ cup almond meal
- ½ cup green apple, peeled and grated
- 4 egg whites
- ¼ cup raw honey or coconut sugar
- ¼ cup almond milk, coconut milk, or water
- 1 tablespoon fresh lemon juice
- ½ teaspoon baking soda
- ¼ teaspoon cinnamon
- ¼ teaspoon salt

Directions:

1. In a large bowl, combine all the ingredients until they are well blended and are the consistency of a pourable batter.

2. Set the batter aside while you heat your frying pan on the stovetop.

3. Spray your frying pan with olive oil cooking spray or coconut oil.

4. Spoon 1/4 cup of the pancake batter into the frying pan and cook on medium-high for 5 minutes on each side.

5. Remove from the pan and eat!

GRAIN-FREE

CEREALS

Coconut Blackberry Bars

Prepackaged snack bars pale in comparison to these fresh and fruity breakfast bars.

Ingredients:

- 1 cup almond flour

- ½ cup unsweetened shredded coconut

- 1 teaspoon cinnamon

- 1 teaspoon baking powder

- ½ teaspoon baking soda

- ½ teaspoon sea salt

- ¼ cup raw honey

- 2 ripe bananas, mashed

- 2 eggs

- 2 tablespoons melted coconut oil or olive oil

- 1 teaspoon pure vanilla extract

- ¾ cup almond or coconut milk

- 1 cup blackberries, fresh or thawed

Directions:

1. Preheat your oven to 350 degrees F.

2. Prepare an 8" × 8" baking pan with coconut spray or olive oil spray and set aside.

3. Using a large bowl, mix together the flour, shredded coconut, cinnamon, baking powder, soda, and salt.

4. Add the honey to this mixture and blend.

5. Now add in the bananas, eggs, oil, vanilla, and 1/4 cup of almond milk.

6. Mix thoroughly until all the ingredients are moist.

7. Be sure the batter has the consistency of a cookie batter. If necessary, add additional amounts of almond milk to achieve this.

8. Gently fold in the blackberries, being careful not to tear them up too much.

9. Spoon the batter into the greased baking pan.

10. Bake for approximately 40 minutes or until the batter is golden brown along the sides.

11. Remove pan from the oven and allow the bars to cool before slicing.

Chocolate Granola Crunch

If you're looking for a handful of crunch, look no further. Great for an energy pick-me-up or an afternoon snack.

Ingredients:

- ½ cup raw sunflower seeds
- ½ cup raw pumpkin seeds
- 1 cup almond meal
- 1 cup unsweetened shredded coconut
- 2 cups raw almonds, slivered or chopped
- 2 tablespoons unsweetened cacao powder
- Pinch of ground cinnamon
- ½ cup coconut oil
- ½ cup raw honey
- 1 teaspoon pure vanilla extract

Directions:

1. Preheat your oven to 325 degrees F.

2. Line a cookie sheet with a piece of aluminum foil that is lightly greased.

3. Take a large mixing bowl and combine the sunflower seeds, pumpkin seeds, almond meal, coconut, almonds, cacao powder, and cinnamon.

4. In a microwave-safe bowl, combine the remaining ingredients of oil, honey, and vanilla.

5. Place the bowl of wet ingredients into the microwave and microwave on high for 20 to 30 seconds to warm it up. This will allow your mixture to pour easily.

6. Place the wet ingredients into the dry ingredients and stir well. Be sure everything is evenly coated.

7. Place the mixture onto your foil-lined cookie.

8. Spread evenly over the cookie sheet.

9. Place the cookie sheet into the oven and bake for 25 minutes, being careful that the mixture doesn't burn. (You may want to stir it once during the process so it cooks evenly).

10. Now remove the cookie sheet from the oven and allow the crunch to cool. You will find this mixture gets crunchy as it gets colder.

11. This recipe can be used in place of a grain cereal by putting it into a bowl with some nut milk or eaten plain.

Cranberry Double Nut Granola

This granola makes an awesome snack for an extra boost of energy. You can eat it plain as a snack or top it with coconut or almond milk for a nutty breakfast cereal.

Ingredients:

- 1 cup of toasted pecans
- 1 cup of toasted sliced almonds
- 1 cup dried unsweetened cranberries
- ¼ - ½ cup unsweetened shredded coconut
- ¼ teaspoon ground cinnamon
- Salt to taste

Directions:

1. Blend all the ingredients in a bowl.
2. Eat plain as a snack or with coconut or almond milk.

SMOOTHIES

&

MORE

Banana Berry Smoothie

Bananas help smoothies create that rich creamy texture that makes a smoothie great. Frozen berries and a spike of ginger are sure to make this a favorite morning drink.

Ingredients:

- 1 ripe banana

- ½ cup frozen berries

- 1 cup of coconut water

- Thumbnail sized piece of fresh ginger, peeled

- 1 teaspoon cinnamon

- 1 tablespoon raw honey

- 2 cups of ice

Directions:

1. Place all the ingredients into a blender.

2. Process on high until a smooth consistency is achieved.

3. Pour into a large glass and enjoy the energy boost.

Berry Nutty Breakfast Smoothie

Finely ground walnuts add a special twist to this berry smoothie. It is really quite refreshing.

Ingredients:

- 1 cup almond or coconut milk or water
- ½ cup frozen berries
- ¼ cup walnuts
- 1 tablespoon raw honey
- 1 teaspoon cinnamon
- 1 cup ice

Directions:

1. Place all the ingredients into a blender.

2. Process on high until a smooth consistency is achieved.

3. Pour into a large glass and enjoy.

Breakfast Sausage

If you have the ability to freshly grind your own meat, this recipe is a great way to use it.

Ingredients:

- 2 pounds ground beef
- 1 pound ground pork
- 2 teaspoons fresh thyme, chopped
- 2 teaspoons fresh sage, chopped
- 1 teaspoon fresh rosemary, chopped
- 2 teaspoons sea salt
- 1½ teaspoons black pepper
- 1 teaspoon fresh grated nutmeg
- ½ teaspoon cayenne

Directions:

1. Begin by combining all of your ingredients in a large mixing bowl.

2. Form the meat mixture into little round balls or links, 1 to 2 inches in diameter.

3. Heat a frying pan or skillet on your stovetop over a medium setting using a small amount of coconut oil in the bottom.

4. Carefully place the meat rounds in the pan and cook for 10 to 15 minutes—until they are browned and cooked through.

5. Remove the meat from the pan and drain any excess oil or grease.

A perfect companion for your pancakes, waffles, or eggs.

Index of Main Ingredients in Recipes

In this index, I have listed some of the main ingredients used in the recipes. If you are new to the Paleo lifestyle, this index will show you some of the ingredients that are often used in recipes. If you have been eating Paleo for quite awhile, some of the ingredients listed in this index will be items you always keep on hand.

Spices and other condiments are not usually referenced here; however, ones like coconut oil and chicken broth are—mostly to help newbies get used to seeing these ingredients. Seldom used items like crabmeat and bacon are mentioned so you can easily find a recipe that uses these ingredients that you may have on hand and others you want to use up.

Under each item, I have included a link to the recipe where that ingredient is used.

Coconut Blackberry Bars   65

~ basil, fresh

Zucchini Pork Casserole   30

~ berries, frozen

Banana Berry Smoothie   73

Berry Nutty Breakfast Smoothie   75

~ blackberries

Coconut Blackberry Bars   65

~ broccoli

Veggie Frittata   12

B.B.C. Frittata   25

~ cacao powder

Almond Banana Bread   43

Chocolate Granola Crunch   68

~ cheese, aged

Quiche Cups   16

B.B.C. Frittata   25

Savory Breakfast Casserole   28

Zucchini Pork Casserole   30

Hearty Morning Egg Cups   35

~ chestnut flour

Nutty Pancakes   55

~ chives, fresh

~ coconut, unsweetened

~ coconut aminos

~ coconut flour

~ coconut milk

~ fruit, dried

~ ginger, fresh

~ ground beef

Chili Crepes	20
Breakfast Sausage	77

~ **honey, raw**

Cranberry Almond Bread	37
Almond Banana Bread	43
Cinnamon Sweet Buns	45
Banana Almond Muffins	47
Nutty Pancakes	55
Fluffy Coconut Pancakes	57
Apple Cinnamon Pancakes	61
Coconut Blackberry Bars	65
Chocolate Granola Crunch	68
Banana Berry Smoothie	73
Berry Nutty Breakfast Smoothie	75

~ **lemon**

Red Pepper & Arugula Omelet	23
Apple Cinnamon Pancakes	61

~ **meat, cooked**

Veggie Frittata	12
Savory Breakfast Casserole	28
Hearty Morning Egg Cups	35

~ **mushrooms**

Garden Fresh Frittata	9
Chili Crepes	20

~ onion

Garden Fresh Frittata	9
Veggie Frittata	12
Chili Crepes	20
Red Pepper & Arugula Omelet	23
Savory Breakfast Casserole	28
Zucchini Pork Casserole	30
Sweet Potato Latkes	59

~ onion, green

Chili Crepes	20

~ parsley

Garden Fresh Frittata	9
South of the Border Frittata	14
Turkey & Eggs	18

~ pecans

Cranberry Double Nut Granola	70

~ pepper, jalapeño

South of the Border Frittata	14

~ pork

Quiche Cups	16
Zucchini Pork Casserole	30
Breakfast Sausage	77

~ pumpkin, 100% canned

Pumpkin Gingerbread Muffins	40

Almond Banana Bread 43

~ pumpkin seeds

Pumpkin Gingerbread Muffins 40

Chocolate Granola Crunch 68

~ pure maple syrup

Pumpkin Gingerbread Muffins 40

~ salsa

South of the Border Frittata 14

~ spinach

Garden Fresh Frittata 9

~ sweet bell peppers

Garden Fresh Frittata 9

Chili Crepes 20

Red Pepper & Arugula Omelet 23

~ sweet potato

South of the Border Frittata 14

Sweet Potato Latkes 59

~ squash

Veggie Frittata 12

~ sunflower seeds

Chocolate Granola Crunch 68

~ tomato, fresh

Red Pepper & Arugula Omelet 23

~ tomato, sun dried

Veggie Frittata	12

~ turkey, ground

Quiche Cups	16
Turkey & Eggs	18

~ walnuts

Cranberry Almond Bread	37
Pumpkin Gingerbread Muffins	40
Berry Nutty Breakfast Smoothie	75

~ zucchini

Zucchini Pork Casserole	30
Cranberry Almond Bread	37

Additional Resources

Gluten-Free Slow Cooker: Easy Recipes for a Gluten Free Diet

Paleolithic Slow Cooker Soups and Stews: Healthy Family Gluten-Free Recipes

Paleo Slow Cooker: Simple and Healthy Gluten-Free Recipes

Going Paleo: A Quick Start Guide for a Gluten-Free Diet

4 MORE Weeks of Fabulous Paleolithic Breakfasts

4 Weeks of Fabulous Paleolithic Lunches

4 Weeks of Fabulous Paleolithic Dinners

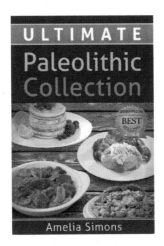

The Ultimate Paleolithic Collection

About the Author

Amelia Simons is a food enthusiast, wife, and mother of five. Frustrated with traditional dieting advice, she stumbled upon the Paleolithic lifestyle of eating and has never looked back. Without bothering to count calories or stress about endless hours of exercise, eating the Paleolithic way enabled Amelia and her husband to effortlessly drop pounds and lower their cholesterol.

Amelia now enjoys sharing the Paleolithic philosophy with friends and readers and finding new ways to turn favorite recipes into healthy alternatives.

Made in the USA
Middletown, DE
16 May 2022